Shoplifting Addiction

The Ultimate Guide for How to Finally Overcome An Addiction to Stealing

Copyright 2015 by Caesar Lincoln - All rights reserved.

This document is geared towards providing exact and reliable information in regards to the topic and issue covered. The publication is sold with the idea that the publisher is not required to render accounting, officially permitted, or otherwise, qualified services. If advice is necessary, legal or professional, a practiced individual in the profession should be ordered.

In no way is it legal to reproduce, duplicate, or transmit any part of this document in either electronic means or in printed format. Recording of this publication is strictly prohibited and any storage of this document is not allowed unless with written permission from the publisher. All rights reserved.

The information provided herein is stated to be truthful and consistent, in that any liability, in terms of inattention or otherwise, by any usage or abuse of any policies, processes, or directions contained within is the solitary and utter responsibility of the recipient reader. Under no circumstances will any legal responsibility or blame be held against the publisher for any reparation, damages, or monetary loss due to the information herein, either directly or indirectly.

The information herein is offered for informational purposes solely, and is universal as so. The presentation of the information is without contract or any type of guarantee assurance.

The trademarks that are used are without any consent, and the publication of the trademark is without permission or backing by the trademark owner. All trademarks and brands within this book are for clarifying purposes only and are the owned by the owners themselves, not affiliated with this document.

Table Of Contents

Introduction

Chapter 1: Understanding Shoplifting

Chapter 2: The Several Faces of Shoplifters

Chapter 3: A Closer Look

Chapter 4: The Kleptomaniac

Chapter 5: The Treatment

Conclusion

Introduction

You will find this short, concise book useful if you make sure to implement what you learn in the following pages. The important thing is that you IMPLEMENT what you learn. A shoplifting addiction is not conquered overnight but the important thing to remember is that it is definitely possible for you to overcome it. The information here is for you to understand your own mind, how a shoplifting addiction negatively affects those around you, as well as the steps you will need to make that journey.

Many people experience shoplifting addiction and are not really aware of the issues that are provoking it. There is a difference between the desire to want things for free and compulsively taking the step to steal items repeatedly. As you go through these pages, you'll develop a better understanding of what shoplifting addiction really is, the research that has been done on shoplifters, and learn several ways that you can overcome it. We will dive into what is going on in your mind, how your body reacts to your triggers, how your early childhood can influence the rest of your life, as well as what work is required of you to get past the roadblocks you have.

It is recommended to take notes while reading this book. This will ensure that you get the most out of the information in here. The notes will help you to pinpoint exactly what you need to implement and by writing things down, you will be able to recall specifics and how to handle certain situations when they arise.

Lastly, it is encouraged that you to do your own research on the topics that you want to look deeper into. The more you understand your own triggers and habits, the better off you will be. To overcome a shoplifting addiction in your life, it will take some work on your part but you can do it! So remember to read with confidence and an open mind!

Chapter 1:

Understanding Shoplifting

Shoplifting is not a new concept developed during contemporary times. Records of shoplifting started appearing during the sixteenth century in London. During that time, which was still three centuries before the Industrial Revolution, urbanization and consumerism were already transforming cities into busy trading centers. According to records during this time, a person caught stealing items worth more than five shillings (equivalent to a fourth of a pound) could be sentenced to death by hanging.

In 1838, the idea that people might not be able to control the urges of shoplifting was seriously given an appropriate amount of attention. French physicians Jean-Etienne Esquirol and

C.C. Marc used the term *"kleptomanie"* to refer to irresistible and involuntary shoplifting (Grant, 2006).

Fast forward to today and shoplifting is among the most prevalent crimes in society. The increasing numbers of cases, resolved and unresolved, are alarming and intriguing; yet, shoplifting receives very little attention in the field of research. Shoplifting is considered, by many people, as a crime and a product of possible psychological disorders.

However, during the 1970s, the same group of people politicized shoplifting as "liberating", transforming the crime into an act of protest. Indeed, there are several interpretations of shoplifting that can be utilized to fully understand the nature of this prevalent social and psychological concern. The lack of studies and research related to shoplifting, however, hinders our full comprehension of the phenomenon.

Although shoplifting is under-researched, there exists a considerable amount of information that can help identify important factors influencing shoplifting as an act and as a disorder.

Shoplifting is defined as theft from the selling floor while a store is open for business (Francis, 1979). This means that if the store was closed or the item in question was not being sold, taking the item without permission or payment is simple "theft". Statistical records reveal the following facts about shoplifting; 1 out of 10 shoppers shoplift (Ray, 1987), 30-40% among adolescents commit the crime repeatedly (Cox, Cox and Moschis, 1990) and 60% of consumers are guilty of shoplifting, at least once, at some point in their lives (Klemke, 1982).

It is somehow unsurprising that shoplifting is so widespread. Ample opportunities are made available by self-service shopping, so that shoplifters can handle goods and conceal them in bags or clothes. Oftentimes, people stealing in shops have the impression that there is little chance for them to get caught. Moreover, once caught, they can still try to get away with the crime by claiming that they honestly forgot about paying for the item.

It appears that people have lesser inhibition about stealing from shops than from an individual. One factor that can be associated with this is the reality that there are deficiencies in shops' stock control. A staff or a retailer is not doing the inventory every minute or every hour; thus, there is little chance for them to notice two or three items missing in their display shelves.

In addition to this, some retailers do not pay much attention to shoplifting, so long as the stolen goods will not amount to more than 2-3% of the total sold goods. As you can imagine, this inability to micro-manage only gets tougher when you start talking about enormous chain retailers that are aiming for rapid national and even global growth. Some of these retailers have hundreds or thousands of people under one roof at the same time.

Most importantly, shoplifting is so prevalent because it can be addicting. This is the reason why shoplifting must not be viewed just as a petty crime but a condition that shoplifters themselves suffer from as well.

According to Klemke (1992), there was a 300% increase in the reported incidents of shoplifting in the past 20 years leading up to 1992. Indeed, the number of shoplifting cases keeps on growing, yet the number of shoplifters caught remains at a very low percentage. According to Griffin (1984), only 1 out of 20-40 shoplifting offenders are apprehended (Krasnovsky & Lane, 1998). This shows that shoplifting, whether intentional or not, remains a huge issue that must be resolved by the authorities or by the owners or management of stores.

Despite the apparent gravity of shoplifting as a psychological disorder or crime and the general disapproving public opinion against it, it does not necessarily mean that the issue will last forever and will remain unresolved. Professionals can help stop individuals, even kleptomaniacs, from shoplifting or other compulsive tendencies. It is possible to tailor each treatment to fit each person's needs. The tips in this book can also be used generally by other individuals to curb the satisfaction of stealing in stores. Although there is no magic pill to stop shoplifting, there is a slow, but steady process to improve one's self.

You Deserve Better

If you are a shoplifter, look at your life right now. Are you satisfied with what you are doing? Do you feel that your life is honorable? Do you see yourself still shoplifting five, or maybe twenty years from now? Needless to say, when you shoplift, you always face the risk of getting caught. You always face the risk of endangering the lives and comfort of the people you love. This does not have to be the case.

You can break your shoplifting addiction. You can solve the problem. Take the challenge and lead the type of life that you deserve. You can be a better person and build yourself up!

Chapter 2:

The Several Faces of Shoplifters

A staff or retailer will never be able to identify who the shoplifters are among a crowd of shoppers, at least at face value. There is just no specific identifying characteristic or avatar of those who aim to steal items in a shop. Stealing, in general, is greatly associated with poverty and sometimes people can identify who is rich and who is poor in a crowd judging by the looks alone. However, in the case of shoplifting, such judgment may not be an effective measure.

There are many people who are stealing items from shops, and poverty is just one of the many factors that might motivate a shoplifter. There are many possible psychological reasons that will motivate a person to shoplift as well. Due to the varying factors triggering the urge of stealing, studies and research were conducted for experts to come up with specific categories that would suffice in addressing these significant differences.

Cameron's Boosters and Snitches

A benchmark study pioneering comprehensive research was conducted by Cameron (1964). The study analyzed shoplifters caught in major department stores in Chicago. Cameron, through this study, was able to identify two major categories of shoplifters, namely, *boosters* and *snitches*. These categories are effective in explaining the behaviors of people who purposely commit the crime. However, you can't use these to explain kleptomaniacs, which will be discussed further in Chapter 4.

The former category, boosters, involve people who shoplift to sell the items later on. These people, who comprised 10% of the population of shoplifters studied by Cameron, have well-defined connections with criminal subdivisions. In essence, boosters are the professional shoplifters. "Fencing" is the term used to describe the crime of reselling stolen goods.

Because of boosters and the advent of online commerce, stores have been pressured to implement stricter security measures against shoplifters. Online auction websites have also taken stricter measures to discourage fencing. Despite this, the crime has become a multi-billion dollar industry, which affects the whole world - especially with the rise of e-commerce.

The latter category, snitches, describes a group of shoplifters that are not stealing to sell. People falling in this category are actually "normal citizens" who are not after the monetary value of the stolen items, but rather choose to use the stolen goods for their own personal purposes. Snitches are often chronic shoplifters, and in Cameron's study, they comprised 90% of the population of shoplifters (Krasnovsky & Lane, 1998).

Moore's Five Categories of Shoplifters

Extending on Cameron's work, Moore, in 1984, identified five categories of shoplifters. Moore used the five dimensions of shoplifting to help identify shoplifting patterns. They include the following:

(1) frequency, or how often the person shoplifts;

(2) primary precipitating factors, or what the major causes are;

(3) use of stolen goods;

(4) attitudes towards shoplifting as a crime; and

(5) reaction to detention, or what they feel in case they get caught and apprehended for shoplifting.

This study revealed five categories of shoplifters, which are *impulse shoplifters, occasional shoplifters, episodic shoplifters, amateur shoplifters,* and *semi-professional shoplifters* (Krasnovsky & Lane, 1998).

Those from the first category, *impulse shoplifters,* are characterized by having limited shoplifting experience (having done the act as little as once or twice). Items that interest them are usually inexpensive, yet tempting, goods such as small baubles, make-up, or food. Stealing from shops is never planned for this group of shoplifters. Once caught, they are usually consumed by embarrassment and guilt, making them unlikely to repeat the offense. Usually, these people only shoplift for the thrill associated with the experience. Oftentimes, they are even fully aware that what they are doing is morally incorrect.

The second group, labeled *occasional shoplifters,* is characterized by committing the crime three to ten times in a year. The reasons behind stealing for this group include complying with peer pressure and economic motivation. In this group, the shoplifters, as much as possible, would not shoplift if the circumstances they were in would not compel them to - or at least this is what they perceive to be their situation.

The third group, *episodic shoplifters,* is reported to include people having psychological problems and severe emotional difficulties. People under this category usually experience strong feelings of guilt and depression. They steal to satisfy an inexplicable personal ritual, which in some way is addressing the strong emotions disturbing the actions. The key difference between episodic shoplifters and occasional shoplifters is that the former is motivated by unwanted personal forces, thus, in most cases they don't have any chance to reject the pressure.

The fourth group, *amateur shoplifters*, is characterized by individuals who decide to repeatedly steal for profit. They usually develop a weekly pattern of shoplifting and develop income streams and rituals. However, they still maintain other activities besides shoplifting, and usually are not doing it because of personal forces like the episodic shoplifters.

Lastly, *semi-professional shoplifters* are characterized as those people who make shoplifting part of their lifestyle. Economic benefits are considered the main motivation for these shoplifters. In addition to this, *semi-professional shoplifters* have the tendency to view themselves as unfairly treated by the immediate society; thus, stealing is done to compensate for the perceived injustice (Krasnovsky & Lane, 1998).

Brady's 16 Shoplifters

One of the most recent works regarding shoplifter behavior was written by forensic psychologist, John Brady. In his book, Why Rich Women Shoplift (2013), Brady identified and examined seven basic psychological aspects that will propel a person to shoplift. Because of the various factors taken into account in his work, Brady's classifications are capable of providing a more complete and rigorous picture of shoplifters.

The first aspect is ***impulse-driven***. This aspect describes how someone can perform the crime solely out of sudden urges. Under this aspect are the Externalizer, the Atypical Shoplifter, and the Compulsive.

The Externalizer is the person who becomes overwhelmed by external forces and is led to perform crime because of an impaired ability to judge moral actions. According to Brady's work, this covers the case of rich women who still shoplift. Their personal circumstances, as well as aggressions, channel through their psyche and shoplifting becomes an expression of their issues.

The Atypical Shoplifter, unlike the Externalizer and Compulsive, has no good reason to shoplift (objectively). Unlike the Compulsive who may still use the shoplifted items for personal gain, the Atypical Shoplifter cannot provide any reason as to why he/she took the item. This classification is the best description of shoplifting out of impulse.

The Compulsive is the person who simply could not control his/her urge to shoplift. This classification is similar to Moore's impulse shoplifter. This type of shoplifter tends to feel extreme feelings of guilt when caught.

The second aspect is ***psychologically motivated***. The shoplifters under this aspect are affected by strong psychological precursors that affect their actions and reasoning. Under this aspect are the Kleptomaniac, the Equalizer, the Trophy Seeker, the Thrill Seeker, the Binge-Spree Shoplifter, and the Situational Shoplifter.

The Kleptomaniac is the most controversial type of shoplifter since he/she is someone who tends to take anything without being fully aware of their actions. Because of its peculiarity, a more detailed discussion is found in Chapter 4.

The Equalizer shoplifts because of past losses. The people under this type feel that life caused them to experience so much loss already - be it loss of loved ones, bankruptcy or other things, and they feel that they have valid justifications to shoplift.

The Trophy Shoplifter is obsessed with having the best type of something - such as the best car, clothes, or cellphones. This type is fueled by being an avid collector, but it may appear that social status also plays a role in being a Trophy Shoplifter.

The Thrill Seeker only shoplifts for the intensity and the excitement that it may bring. This type shoplifts because it gives the person a kick or a high out of the act. Because of this, most thrill seekers are adolescents or even young adults.

The Binge-Spree Shoplifter behaves to impress peers. Similar to sporadic and reckless bursts of drinking or gambling, the Binge-Spree Shoplifter is usually compelled by small but numerous external influences. Because of these, Binge-Spree Shoplifters are usually teenagers.

The Situational Shoplifter is, simply put, an opportunist. When the opportunity presents itself to take something that excites the person with little chance of being caught, the Situational Shoplifter will steal the item.

The third aspect is ***economically influenced***. This describes all precursors that are concerned with status or money. The types under this aspect are the Professional and the Economically Disadvantaged Shoplifter.

On one hand, the Professional Shoplifter steals for profit, and is identical to Cameron's boosters. This person is fully conscious of his/her actions and will not feel guilty when caught. On the other hand, the Economically Disadvantaged Shoplifter will shoplift basic necessities. Unlike the former, he/she will possibly feel guilty when caught, but will still feel a sense of anger towards an unfair society that makes him/her feel forced to shoplift to get by.

The fourth aspect is **age determined**. There is only one type of shoplifter under this aspect, and that is the Provisional/Delinquent. There is an emerging trend among adolescents of antisocial, aggressive, or anti-establishment behaviors. This trend causes some teenagers to shoplift in an attempt to appear "edgy".

The fifth aspect is **alcohol and substance connected**. Substance abuse is a factor frequently associated with shoplifting. Studies show a positive relationship between substance abuse and stealing. The Drug/Alcohol Addict steals to be able to fund a chosen form of addiction.

The sixth aspect is **mentally or medically impaired**. Because of troubles in their mental health, people affected by this aspect are almost aways never in the proper state of mind. The types under this aspect are the Alzheimer's Sufferer or Amnesiac and the Chemically/Alcohol Driven Shoplifter.

The Alzheimer's Sufferers or Amnesiacs are classified as shoplifters because they walk out of the store forgetting to pay for the items they brought with them. This type becomes more and more common since the people who suffer from these symptoms come from an older age group. At the advent of medical advancement, the average age of death continues to rise, and more people are prone to becoming this type of shoplifter.

The Chemically/Alcohol Driven Shoplifter is already under the influence of liquor or drugs that impair his/her judgment. Because of this, the person is different from the Drug/Alcohol Addict because the latter steals to get more access to the item(s) they are addicted to. The Chemically/Alcohol Driven Shoplifter may not have any reasonable cause to shoplift.

The seventh and last aspect ***has no identifiable psychosocial drivers***. The only type under this aspect is the Inadvertent/Amateur Shoplifter. Unlike Moore's definition of Amateur shoplifters, this type simply describes people who have simply forgotten to pay for an item and have walked away with a stolen good. We can't expect them to feel guilty or not; their response to being caught or whether or not they will return the item is completely up to them.

Other Types of Shoplifters

Other studies on shoplifting have also revealed specific classifications of the people who engage in the act. A team headed by Schlueter categorized shoplifters into *rational, non-rational,* and *mixed. Rational shoplifters* were identified as those who have clear goals in mind when shoplifting, while *non-rational* shoplifters are those who seem to be motivated by immediate desire or need. Mixed shoplifters exhibit any of the mentioned properties at a given time, thus, they are more complicated to understand (Schlueter, O'Neal, Hickey & Sellers, 1989).

Another study conducted by Arboleda-Florez and colleagues (1977) revealed three categories of shoplifters. First on the list is the *snitch* group, which includes people who are not after the monetary value of the items stolen. The second category is called *unusual.* People who fall under this category are described as motivated by hostility prompted by emotionally charged interpersonal problems. The third and last category is *psychotic*. This group includes shoplifters who, during the shoplifting act, experience delusions (Krasnovsky & Lane, 1998).

There are several other classifications used to characterize the varying nature and personalities of the shoplifters. Nonetheless, what's evident is that shoplifting is often associated with some forms of psychological disturbance. Whatever label is given, whether it's called impulsive, episodic, unusual, psychotic, or non-rational, one thing remains certain: these people do not just need legal intervention, but psychological help as well.

In a study conducted by Cupchik and Atcheson (1983) with shoplifters who were referred for some form of psychological help, it was found that most cases of shoplifting were precipitated by personal loss or anticipation of such loss.

These cases include the death of a loved one, loss of health, loss of a relationship, and loss in others aspects of life (Krasnovsky & Lane, 1998).

Losing something or someone might be considered one of the heaviest encumbrances a person could carry in his/her life. Thus, some people find it difficult to keep up with whatever changes the loss would bring into their lives. Coping can be difficult for some and sometimes the things they do to soothe their strong emotional disturbances are more felonious than therapeutic. Another way of looking at the situation is that the shoplifters, under extreme psychological stress, acquire objects they might possibly need for the incoming event.

As researchers suggest, shoplifting is used by some people to respond to compulsion prompted by their psychological disturbance. This is the reason why even rich, well-respected icons in society can still fall victim to the petty crime of shoplifting.

Studies also reveal that aside from "loss", shoplifters are influenced by psychiatric history, having low self-esteem and experiences of family or marital conflict. Needless to say, the reasons behind the act of shoplifting can be products of complex factors. Playing a pivotal role, nonetheless, is the poor coping mechanism in dealing with psycho-social stressors.

Some women suffering from eating disorders like anorexia and bulimia are also engaged in shoplifting as studies suggest. The items stolen in these cases are highly related to the eating disorder experienced (like food and laxatives) and the reason for stealing includes the avoidance of embarrassment produced by purchasing the said products.

What type of shoplifter are you? Knowledge of your type can give you a clear idea on what aspects of your life you need to improve on or address. This is one of the first steps you must take before fully reconciling with yourself and changing for the better.

Chapter 3:

A Closer Look

The concept of shoplifting proposes many interesting questions. Why do people do it? How are they affected? Who else can become affected whenever someone shoplifts? So far, we have mostly treated shoplifting as an isolated phenomenon in a sense that we mostly talked about the shoplifter alone. This chapter will attempt to probe deeper into the mind of the shoplifter, as well as examine the effects of the crime on the life of the person, of the people in his/her immediate vicinity, and the people in the community at large.

Some consider shoplifting as a way to make things right for the unfairness that they perceive in the society that they live in. In this case, being able to materialize revenge brings some sort of fulfillment to the person performing the act.

Young people usually steal from shops for the excitement of undergoing and completing a challenge. Adolescents enjoy the thrill brought about by doing something deviant and getting away with it unnoticed. There is speculation that this is brought about by anti-establishment punk, emo, and rap culture, which is popular among adolescents. These cultures promote deviant and destructive behavior, as seen in music videos, fashion, or even political statements on the internet or on the streets.

Because of the widespread reach of information through the internet, these two cultures can heavily influence the youth. However, we must be careful with this argument, as it opens the can of worms to the debate of whether parents should do a better job raising their children, instead of blaming popular culture and prevalent musicians for the actions of the children. Regardless of which side one takes, it is important to consider all triggers in this case. Whatever the reason pushing a person to turn to shoplifting, there is a huge probability that the associations made among the factors involved will later on result in addiction.

Another key to a shoplifter's mind is that a person suffering from shoplifting addiction will tend to have repetitive thoughts about it. Consistently, a person's mind will be bugged by tension and pressure that is "conditioned" to be relieved only by the act of shoplifting. This type of conditioning is common among sufferers of kleptomania.

As a crime, shoplifting is not considered to be a major concern; however, as a psychological disorder, shoplifting must be given appropriate attention. Shoplifting addiction carries similar characteristics to people that are addicted to a substance. Anyone can develop this kind of addiction, although vulnerability can be heightened by psychiatric history or existing emotional disturbances.

The following sections show you additional reasons why it is necessary to stop your shoplifting addiction in its tracks. Remember that shoplifting is a crime, and it can affect many people regardless of how little of an act we perceive it to be.

Shoplifting and the Economy

Why is shoplifting a crime? In modern society, trade fuels the backbone of the economy. Companies rely on their products to generate profit, and the market needs innovative products for consumers to buy. The state or government recognizes the role of stores in stimulating the economy and providing its citizens their needs, among other things. This is why shoplifting is considered a crime.

The state reassures the stores and companies under it that their products are protected, so that they can potentially give a good return on investment. This is one of the state's ways to empower stores and companies so that they can further improve the economy.

In a dystopian society where shoplifting is rampant and unchallenged, companies will become more and more discouraged to produce items to be sold to the market. Regardless of your reasons for shoplifting or your opinions regarding big companies and their profit-driven operations, you must always be able to respect the prices they set through purchasing their products.

It is unfair that we steal from companies. Shoplifting is a losing proposition because it disrespects the confidence companies have in their customers. Once they gradually stop producing, we, the average consumer, will be the ones at a loss.

How Shoplifting Can Ruin Your Life

Once you understand your shoplifting habits by personally resonating with one of the provided categories in Chapter 2, you can better understand the possible causes behind your compulsion. However, understanding the reasons is not enough. Without action, your addiction can significantly affect your life and the lives of the people around you, especially of those you love.

First and foremost, you are the most affected person when your shoplifting addiction goes unchecked. There are two ways to look at it. For one, you allow your body and mind to maintain and cultivate whatever is causing you to shoplift. Also, you expose yourself directly to numerous risks.

As for the first part, we have already covered the many faces of shoplifters. There is almost always a psychological or physiological reason why one continues to take items without paying. For the former, a person may feel extreme stress, peer pressure, angst, greed, or may be experiencing a severe mental condition.

For the latter, a person may be under the influence of drugs or liquor. Although we have not covered everything that could trigger shoplifting, all of these mentioned are severe issues that take control of your life and prohibit you from functioning properly or being fully happy. When you continue to shoplift, you are validating these hindrances. You sink further into your own demise and, overall, you are not helping yourself to become a more productive member of society.

Secondly, and this is especially true for people who shoplift to get by, the addiction will most likely cause you to face serious jail time. Always remember that shoplifting is a crime, and crimes always have punishments. Although for minor instances of shoplifting only a fine will be charged, the fines will surely rack up if you continue doing it.

If the authorities retrieve evidence of your shoplifting activity, they will most likely believe you are also capable of stealing large amounts or items of really great value. When you shoplift more expensive items, the punishment will be greater, and you will most likely end up in jail. This is not a pleasant experience. As much as possible, do not allow yourself to be led to jail over something you can have control over.

Harm does not only apply to yourself. Since shoplifting is a crime, it will definitely also affect your community, specifically your family and friends. According to Dan Lewis and Michael Maxfield (1980), the fear of crime of people living in the neighborhood is heavily influenced by the environment they are in. When you participate in shoplifting, you are also introducing risk to your community. You contribute to making your neighborhood a less safe place to live in.

The worst part of this scenario is when close family members, especially children, become aware of your shoplifting tendencies. They'll then view shoplifting as something normal and an activity that they too can partake in, since you yourself can do it effortlessly. Understand that you are part of a much larger community. You can influence other people with your behavior. With the emerging trends of shoplifting among the youth, you should stop yourself before you negatively affect the lives of others.

If you cannot stop your shoplifting addiction for your own benefit, then please consider doing it for other people. Many lives are potentially affected when you participate in this act. Looking at shoplifting closely, it is an intricate crime with vast sociological consequences. Before you act, realize the power of your crime. It may not be the most serious crime in the world, but it is a crime nonetheless.

Chapter 4:

The Kleptomaniac

Kleptomania is a psychological disorder characterized by uncontrollable and repetitive stealing of items not needed for personal consumption (Grant, 2006). Similar to shoplifting addiction, studies and research about kleptomania are very few in number and depth. Because of this, the whole of Chapter 4 is dedicated to uncover and explain the details of kleptomania. Also, since kleptomania is different from ordinary shoplifting addiction, we'll also cover current treatment strategies for kleptomania. Treatment options for the other forms of shoplifting are presented in Chapter 5.

Throughout the history of the scientific literature, kleptomania was only mentioned in an episodic manner. This means that although we can describe some people as kleptomaniacs, we do not expect that they will always take things with them. Although the said disorder can be found in the very first Diagnostic and Statistical Manual of Mental Disorders (DSM-l), it was not recorded as a distinct diagnosis, but as a supplementary term instead.

Kleptomania is characterized by the following;

(1) recurrent failure to resist impulses to steal objects that are not needed for personal use or for their monetary value;

2) increasing sense of tension immediately before committing the theft;

3) pleasure, gratification, or relief at the time of committing the theft;

4) the stealing is not committed to express anger or vengeance and is not in response to a delusion or a hallucination; and

5) the stealing is not better accounted for by conduct disorder, a manic episode, or antisocial personality disorder (Grant, 2006).

Historically, because of the first criterion, kleptomania was believed to be a disorder for women in the upper or upper-middle class. This was true because only these demographics could have taken items without paying but actually had the means to pay them. People of other demographics, especially those who have lesser means to pay for taken items, were just interpreted to have been "stealing".

Although we now have a better understanding of race, gender, roles, and psychology, many of us still carry the stigma that kleptomania is a disorder normally found in wealthy women with an abundance of time and resources.

Studies regarding kleptomania reveal that people who suffer from this disorder have had experienced riotous and an unusually stressful childhood. Also, kleptomaniacs are found to have the symptoms of anxiety and/or depression. In addition to these, people who suffer from kleptomania usually have experienced social isolation, marital turmoil, and/or low self-esteem.

The Stigma of Kleptomania

Kleptomania is one of the most difficult cases of shoplifting because people generally understand that it is a mental condition. For sufferers of this disorder, it is difficult to fit in, have other people understand you, or feel at ease in social situations.

According to a study lead by Azhar (2015), when people hear that someone is a kleptomaniac, they are more likely to carry negative stigma than before, when they were not aware of a specific label for the individual in question. This clearly shows how the public needs to be better educated regarding the implications and reactions towards kleptomania.

In general, people are afraid of those with mental illnesses. In a British study, survey respondents showed to have a negative bias against people with mental illnesses such as schizophrenia, alcoholism, or drug abuse. The public generally views them as dangerous and unpredictable, and believes that it is the fault of the person with the mental illness, as to why other people think of them in that way.

The respondents also showed that they think people with disorders are difficult to communicate with (Crisp *et al.*, 2000). Because of these negative stigmas, those with mental illnesses, including those who also have kleptomaniac tendencies, become socially isolated, discriminated upon, and easily distressed, especially when dealing with other people in a position of authority such as employers.

If you are a kleptomaniac, do not worry. Do not let the opinions of others affect you, because they do not truly understand the situation. However, they should motivate you to understand your condition and work to get yourself treated.

Occurrence and Diagnosis

The main reason why scientific research on kleptomania is scarce is because it is a rare problem. According to studies, only around six to eight people in every one thousand can be classified as kleptomaniacs (Dannon, 2002; Goldman, 1992; Lepkifker *et al.*, 1999). However, up to eight kleptomaniacs can be found per one hundred individuals undergoing mental clinical treatment (Grant, 2006).

This disorder has been a highly misunderstood issue for the longest time, thus, those affected by it continually suffer. Historically, people have reduced it to mere theft or to other disorders, such as addiction or obsessive-compulsiveness. Up until now, it is clear that it is poorly understood.

However, it is evident to researchers that symptoms of kleptomania almost always come with other mental conditions. Doctors can diagnose kleptomania better if other relevant factors, such as increased stress, social isolation, and impaired cognition, also occur. It is unclear as to whether kleptomania causes these other mental symptoms or if it emerges because of them.

Argued Causes and Assessments of Kleptomania

There have been more attempts to understand kleptomania in the last 20 years. Many psychologists tried fusing Sigmund Freud's psychoanalytic models with biological models. Because of these, experts describe the sensation of kleptomania as craving the sensation of fulfilling stimulus (taking an item). This action causes changes in the brain.

With repeated fulfillment of kleptomaniac tendencies, called as a behavioral chain, bolder and harder to resist tendencies can form. For example, a kleptomaniac develops thoughts that he/she could get away with stealing an item earlier on in the behavioral chain (Kohn & Antonuccio, 2002). Later in the chain, the kleptomaniac may simply take anything at all, without any regards for the item(s) or circumstance.

Kleptomania is often understood as the collection of unwanted traits that result from respondent and operant conditioning, shaping, distorted cognitions, behavioral chaining, and poor coping skills (Gauthier & Pellerin, 1982). The understanding of kleptomania's multiple sources eliminates the need to identify a single point where it must have begun, thus, allowing treatment to begin much sooner.

To assess the possibility of kleptomania among suspected individuals, questionnaires are useful for professionals who wish to discover the actual causes and outcomes of an individual's kleptomaniac behavior. With the retrieved data, the testers can study whether an individual's tendencies match up with other known factors, such as tendencies for obsessive compulsiveness.

Kleptomania Treatment

Sadly, there has not yet been any wide attempt of performing treatment studies for kleptomania. While other mental illnesses that may appear with kleptomania, such as obsessive compulsive disorder, are treated with medicine, kleptomania itself cannot be treated with medicine just yet.

The current body of knowledge concerning medication and kleptomania have produced varied results and unwanted side effects. Professionals currently believe that medication should vary with the type of kleptomania someone has. Therefore, professionals are currently studying the various antecedents and consequences of the disorder.

The current employed approaches to treat kleptomania are largely behavioral. For example, individuals are expected to describe aloud a certain kleptomaniac situation in clear detail. The level of anxiety increases all throughout as the individual is forced to describe being caught, hearing the court trial decision, or being sent to jail. Doing this repeatedly over multiple sessions can greatly decrease kleptomaniac tendencies.

This exercise can be done in the comfort of your own bed. Focus on visualization in your mind, drawing out the scenes in which you could find yourself in, and journaling your thoughts on the potential consequences. This can be very powerful in curbing or eliminating your behavior!

However, one must couple it with various other treatment options such as homework or behavioral chaining. Because of the difficulty of treatment and the need to process gradual progress, kleptomania treatment is recommended to be performed by professionals.

Chapter 5:

The Treatment

The impression that shoplifting is not really a serious crime somehow influences the very little amount of research aimed at assessing treatments for shoplifters. The blurred lines between shoplifting as a crime and as a psychological condition might be influencing the fact that some researchers do not see shoplifting as a worthy social problem. Even people outside the research field rated shoplifting's seriousness as a crime to be very low (Krasnovsky & Lane, 1998).

Apprehension is enough for some shoplifters to stop the act completely, especially for those who never considered themselves thieves prior to the shoplifting incident. However, for the case of shoplifting addicts, even some jail time will not immediately halt their unusual cravings to steal.

As far as the mental effects, shoplifting addiction is similar to other forms of addiction. Living with the presence of very strong urges to perform the act will not allow someone to sleep peacefully at night. The stealing must be done to achieve satisfaction. Having these experiences will really make a person and his/her relationships suffer. Thus, in all shoplifting addicts there is always a part of them that wants to get out of such a dire situation and it is obviously ruining their lives.

The very first key to address shoplifting addiction is to admit that there is something wrong. This is very basic and simple, yet it is the most difficult part for some people. Admitting that one needs help is never easy considering that most shoplifters are not willing to admit guilt of such acts, especially in front of other people. Shoplifters will generally and continually find reasons to justify their shoplifting. They should stop this mentality and come to terms with the idea that shoplifting is a crime in the first place.

Shoplifting addiction is such a secretive thing that almost nobody among the people experiencing the disorder will see a doctor and fess up about their stealing habit. A person can actually carry the addiction for several years without his/her friends knowing about it, unless apprehended publicly. Nevertheless, any form of compulsive actions or addictions are not healthy and must be appropriately addressed. To be able to halt the addiction, one must be able to admit and be willing to submit to some help.

Shoplifting addiction might be triggered by different factors; thus, one must be able to pinpoint which among the possible factors has caused his/her shoplifting behavior. Knowing the cause (root) is the most effective way to address the problem.

Observing the stealing patterns and keeping a record book regarding the experiences will help one evaluate his/her own compulsive behaviors. Only by writing down one's shoplifting activity every time it happens will a person become fully aware of the entirety of the events. This step will allow an individual to see the bigger picture, which includes important details that are significant to understanding the patterns.

A vivid description of the emotions felt before, during, and after the shoplifting experience is necessary to be included in the record book. These events are of utmost importance to root out precipitating factors. The triggers that you feel which cause you to make the decision to go through with the act, are key here.

Be sure to pay attention to how different events/people affect your emotional state throughout the day. You will begin to see patterns, for example, you might be more likely to steal when you have a disagreement with your family. Maybe you tend to steal when you are stressed out from work or feel pressure financially. Pay attention to these factors and over weeks and months, you will be able to see what influences your actions from an objective point of view.

Another action that one must do is to re-read all entries on a weekly or daily basis (depending on the frequency and severity of the stealing) and to come up with a reflection journal entry about how he/she feels after reading what he/she wrote days ago.

Many times, people can not believe that they do the things they have actually been doing. People have the tendency to see their acts in a lighter manner than how it actually is being perceived in reality. By embracing this step, one's self-awareness will be widened and the actions will be seen more objectively in their own mind.

The next step is reality checking. A person addicted to shoplifting must have full awareness of all the possible consequences of the act. The possibilities must be listed in the journal/record book and the list must not be limited to short term effects. What will happen in the next 10 years? How about the next 20 years? Assessing long term effects is as significant as understanding short term ones. By realizing that a behavior serves no purpose in your life ten years from now, you'll start to see it as a time waster.

Aiming to change for the benefit of one's self is important; nonetheless, dedicating to other people like family or friends, one's efforts to change will give him/her an additional driving force from within. Shoplifting addiction, just like any other form of addiction, can destroy personal and social relationships. A person who is suffering from shoplifting addiction has probably felt the negative effects of the crime in his/her life. Aside from his/her own self, significant others will be hurt and will suffer as well. Realizing this will give a person a loud wake up call.

The key here is to really put yourself in a position where you can feel the consequences as if they are happening now. Close your eyes and begin to visualize and feel the pain your future mistakes will have on those around you if you allow your addiction to continue. By internalizing these feelings, you will begin to think differently when shoplifting opportunities present themselves.

Distracting one's self is another effective way to address shoplifting addiction. The addiction happens because of several different triggering factors. So what one must do is to distract the self with another (and this time healthy) activity. Sometimes people become addicted to stealing because they feel powerful and in control in the process. If this is the case, then one must find healthy hobbies that will make him/her feel dominant and in control.

One way to accomplish this is to discover a person's talent or special quirks or abilities, something that he/she is proficient and interested in. For instance, if a person enjoys painting then he/she can keep themselves busy with this activity. In painting, a person holds power over what will be seen in the canvas. The artist is in control over the details and techniques of putting elements together to come up with a work of art.

Dealing with shoplifting addiction alone is possible; nonetheless, the process will not be easy for most. It is best to ask help from other people. Having more than one perspective to plan and see the behavior modification process through will make the treatment more feasible. If there is a group of people who will surely understand and will genuinely offer help, it would be one's family and close friends. Therefore, one must be brave enough to share his/her shoplifting addiction problem with at least one close associate.

Just the mere fact that one feels heard and acknowledged will make him/her feel better. Significant others might be of great help in observing behavioral patterns of the person addicted to shoplifting. An outsider's perspective will help keep the observation and date gathering more holistic in nature. In the absence of any family member, the closest and most trusted friend can be the person a shoplifting addict could turn to.

Seeking professional help will also aid a person suffering from shoplifting addiction. Counseling coming from a psychologist or psychiatrist is the best help if the person cannot open up about the problem with his/her family and friends. If a person is too afraid that people around him/her will suddenly change once they have learned about his/her addiction to stealing, then a professional therapist is the best person one can turn to. A professional can also identify if there are other psychological problems a person is experiencing, aside from the addiction.

The key to remember is that if you feel too isolated to bring up the issue with your family or close friends, you must pursue the professional counseling route. Having at least one other person to be accountable to is an integral part of the process. And remember that they are paid to be that source for you. Do not feel ashamed to go to them, as they probably deal with people on a daily basis who have done worse things than you.

Joining shoplifting-specific treatment programs can also help people addicted to shoplifting. Knowing that there are other people with the same condition will make a person less anxious about his/her condition. Undergoing the healing process together with other hopefuls might encourage a person to take the program more seriously. Furthermore, by joining such groups, a person can be exposed to first-hand information on how others were able to curb and control their impulses. The stories that will be shared by other people can offer inspiring thoughts and can serve as a way for a person to learn vicariously.

Medical treatment is also available to help people suffering from shoplifting addiction. Naltrexone is a drug that is commonly prescribed to treat people with heroin and alcohol addiction. Now this drug is also being used to help treat shoplifting addiction by some doctors.

One thing that must not be forgotten is the reality that there is no easy way out. Shoplifting addiction is similar to other forms of addiction; therefore, one must not expect a smooth-flowing transition from being addicted to sobering up to being fully healed. It will take a lot of effort, willingness, time, encouragement, desire, and motivation to get through the process. Nevertheless, hope never fails a strong-willed heart!

Conclusion

You don't have to rush in curbing your shoplifting addiction, since it is more advisable to do it in a gradual, yet guaranteed process. If there is anything you should take from the knowledge and information presented in this book, it is that shoplifting can severely and negatively affect you, your family, your community and your country. This does not need to be so. Keep your head high, and commit to becoming a better person.

The next thing to do is to make sure you are actively following your treatment plan and tracking your progress. Be very committed to journaling your experiences in a notebook. Confide in a close friend, family member, or lover. Feel the difference whenever you successfully say no to your urges to shoplift, and celebrate them! Being aware of these will motivate you to do continue with your recovery.

Hopefully this short, concise book has given you a healthier, more well-rounded perspective on a common, yet misunderstood phenomenon. Whether you are a shoplifter, know of someone who engages in shoplifting, or just interested in the topic, good luck in your own journey!

Works Cited:

Abodela-Florez, J., Durie, H., & Costello, J. (1977). Shoplifting-An Ordinary Crime? *International Journal of Offender Therapy and Comparative Criminology*, 201-208.

Azhar, H. Mohamed, K. Perera, A. Siddiqua, A., Ferreira, N., Hyland, L. Pietschnig, J. (2015). Attitudes Towards Mental Illnesses: Effects of Labels and Associations with Materialism. Gulf Medical Journal.

Brady, J.C. (2013). *Why Rich Women Shoplift – When They Have It All*. San Jose, CA: Western Psych Press.

Cameron, M. O. (1964). *The Booster and the Snitch: Department Store Shoplifting*. New York: Free Press of Glencoe.

Crisp, A. H., Gelder, M. G., Rix, S., Meltzer, H. I., & Rowlands, O. J. (2000). Stigmatisation of people with mental illnesses. *The British Journal of Psychiatry*, *177*(1), 4-7.

Dannon, P. (2003). Topiramate for the treatment of kleptomania: A case series and review of the literature. Clinical Neuropharmacology, 26, 1-4.

Gauthier, J., & Pellerin, D. (1982). Management of compulsive shoplifting through covert sensitization. Journal of Behavior Therapy and Experimental Psychiatry, 13, 73-75.

Goldman, M. J. (1992). Kleptomania: An overview. Psychiatric Annals, 22, 68-71.

Grant, J. E. (2006). Understanding and TreatingKleptomania:NewModels and. *Isr J Psychiatry Relat Sci*, 81-87.

Kohn, C. S., & Antonuccio, D. O. (2002). Treatment of kleptomania using cognitive and behavioral strategies. Clinical Case Studies, 1, 25-38.

Krasnovsky, T., & Lane, R. C. (1998). Shoplifting: A Review of the Literature. *Aggression and Violent Behavior*, 219-235.

Lepkifker, E., Dannon, P. N. & Ziv, R., Iancu, I., Horesh, N., & Kotler, M. (1999). The treatment of kleptomania with serotonine reuptake inhibitors. Clinical Neuropharmacology, 22, 40-43.

Lewis, D. A., & Maxfield, M. G. (1980). Fear in the neighborhoods: An investigation of the impact of crime. *Journal of research in crime and delinquency, 17*(2), 160-189.

Made in the USA
Monee, IL
05 December 2019